Jumpstarters for Synonyms and Antonyms

Short Daily Warm-ups for the Classroom

By
LINDA ARMSTRONG

COPYRIGHT © 2011 Mark Twain Media, Inc.

ISBN 978-1-58037-571-9

Printing No. CD-404149

Mark Twain Media, Inc., Publishers
Distributed by Carson-Dellosa Publishing LLC

Visit us at www.carsondellosa.com

Table of Contents

Introduction to the Teacher

In today's competitive environment, effective verbal skills are more essential than ever. A rich, precise vocabulary is the most important instrument in any communicator's toolbox. Reading and discussion remain the most effective ways to build vocabulary, but classroom practice can help.

This book offers teachers and parents short warm-up activities to help young readers and writers develop verbal proficiency by working with synonyms and antonyms. When used at the beginning of language arts, mathematics, science, spelling, geography, or health and safety time-slots, these mini-tasks offer students opportunities to become familiar with useful new words.

Units Feature Adjectives, Adverbs, Verbs, and Nouns

Descriptive words are often used to point out similarities and differences. For this reason, many of the most common synonyms and antonyms are modifiers. The adjectives and adverbs featured in this Jumpstarters collection describe qualities, emotions, and relative locations.

Many nouns and verbs also have synonyms and antonyms. Action words and object names are covered in separate sections.

Note: Some of the words included in this book are familiar. Others are very challenging. Dictionaries will help students complete the more difficult exercises.

> Before distributing the exercises, explain that **synonyms** are words with similar meanings and **antonyms** are words with opposite meanings. Encourage students to notice that some words have several meanings with different sets of synonyms and antonyms.

Many Ways to Use This Book

- Reproduce the pages, cut along the lines, and use each section as a ten-minute warm-up or part of a homework assignment.
- Distribute copies of uncut pages so students can keep their completed exercises in a three-ring binder for reference.
- For use at a learning center, reproduce each page, cut the exercises apart, and mount each on a card with the corresponding answer key section on the back. Laminate for durability.
- Make transparencies or PowerPoint™ slides for group lessons
- Share the exercises in any order that fits your ongoing program.

Ideas for Additional Practice

- Encourage students to notice synonyms and antonyms in texts, novels, periodicals, and even advertisements.
- Crossword puzzles are great tools for vocabulary development. They often use synonyms or antonyms as clues.
- Latin and Greek roots are powerful vocabulary-development tools. Prefixes and suffixes such as *un-* and *-tion* are also important. Lists are available online.
- Some students find a personal dictionary useful. When they encounter a new word, they enter it in a composition book fitted with alphabetical tabs. They write the word and a brief definition, along with synonyms and antonyms.

Synonyms and Antonyms Warm-ups: Part I Qualities; Adjectives Related to Size

Name/Date _____

Adjectives Related to Size 1

Unscramble the synonym for each word.

1. small   tllite _____
2. tiny   umnvetidii _____
3. huge   cngitiga _____
4. average   yalptic _____
5. big   agrel _____

Name/Date _____

Adjectives Related to Size 2

Fill in the antonym's missing letters.

1. medium   e __ tr __ me
2. great   t __ __ y
3. microscopic g __ ga __ tic
4. colossal   m __ n __ s __ __ le
5. large   s __ a __ __

Name/Date _____

Adjectives Related to Size 3

Circle the best synonym for the first word in each line.

1. intermediate: huge   middle   diminutive
2. diminutive: little   intermediate   enormous
3. bulky: compact   average   massive
4. enormous: intermediate immense   infinitesimal
5. miniature: minuscule   giant   intermediate

Name/Date _____

Adjectives Related to Size 4

On your own paper, use each pair of antonyms in a sentence.

1. minute/enormous
2. gigantic/tiny
3. minuscule/gargantuan
4. bulky/compact
5. massive/infinitesimal

Name/Date _____

Adjectives Related to Size 5

Cross out the word that is not a synonym for the first word in each line.

1. mammoth: gargantuan   minuscule
2. gigantic: microscopic   immense
3. massive: mammoth   infinitesimal
4. gargantuan: diminutive   colossal
5. infinitesimal: mammoth   microscopic

Synonyms and Antonyms Warm-ups: Part I Qualities; Adjectives Related to Shape

Name/Date _____

Adjectives Related to Shape 1

Circle the best synonym for the first word in each line.

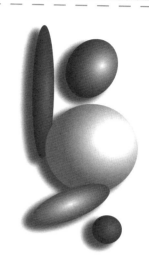

1. round: circular   quadrilateral   triangular
2. square: circular   boxy   triangular
3. narrow: extensive   circular   thin
4. wide: thick   constricted   threadlike
5. flat: spherical   constricted   level

Name/Date _____

Adjectives Related to Shape 2

Unscramble the synonym for each word.

1. circular   udnro _____
2. blocky   cciub _____
3. rotund   ppuml _____
4. globular   hicaerspl _____
5. curved   wedbo _____

Name/Date _____

Adjectives Related to Shape 3

Fill in the synonym's missing letters.

1. rectangular   qu __ d __ il __ __ er __ l
2. spherical   gl __ __ ul __ r
3. cubic   b __ o __ __ y
4. slender   s __ __ __ __
5. thin   na __ __ __ w

Name/Date _____

Adjectives Related to Shape 4

Circle *synonyms* or *antonyms* to identify each word pair.

1. thick/thin   synonyms antonyms
2. level/flat   synonyms antonyms
3. spherical/globular   synonyms
                                     antonyms
4. slender/rotund   synonyms antonyms

Name/Date _____

Adjectives Related to Shape 5

Circle T for True or F for False.

T F   1. If something is *round*, it is *quadrilateral*.
T F   2. If something is *conical*, it is *pyramidal*.
T F   3. If a box is *hollow*, it is *solid*.
T F   4. The opposite of *thinning* is *widening*.
T F   5. One antonym of *pointed* is *dull*.

Synonyms and Antonyms Warm-ups: Part I Qualities; Adjectives Related to Age

Name/Date _____

Adjectives Related to Age 1

Circle *synonyms* or *antonyms* to identify each word pair.

1. old/elderly   synonyms   antonyms
2. young/youthful   synonyms   antonyms
3. new/ancient   synonyms   antonyms
4. fresh/novel   synonyms   antonyms
5. stale/fresh   synonyms   antonyms

Name/Date _____

Adjectives Related to Age 2

On your own paper, use each pair of antonyms in a sentence.

1. ancient/modern
2. elderly/young
3. current/outdated
4. archaic/recent
5. fashionable/outmoded

Name/Date _____

Adjectives Related to Age 3

Unscramble the synonym for each word.

1. contemporary rnrecut _____
2. present   nartemcoypor _____
3. outmoded   onfauhislenab _____
4. antique   onatrtiadil _____
5. primordial   aimelprv _____

Name/Date _____

Adjectives Related to Age 4

Fill in the antonym's missing letters.

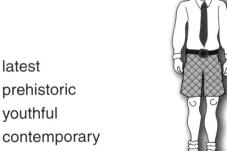

1. modern   an __ i __ nt
2. prehistoric   mo __ __ r n
3. unsullied   d __ __ a __ __ d
4. obsolete   ad __ a __ __ ed
5. innovative   un __ r __ g __ nal

Name/Date _____

Adjectives Related to Age 5

Circle the synonym for the first word in each line.

1. recent: antique   archaic   latest
2. renewed: improved   obsolete   prehistoric
3. antediluvian: modern   ancient   youthful
4. unfashionable: outmoded   innovative   contemporary
5. archaic: present   modern   antiquated

Synonyms and Antonyms Warm-ups: Part I Qualities; Adjectives Related to Strength

Name/Date _____

Adjectives Related to Strength 1

Cross out the choice that is not an antonym for the first word in the line.

1. strong: vigorous   feeble
2. weak: powerful   feeble
3. vigorous: sluggish   forceful
4. intense: extreme   ordinary
5. feeble: listless   robust

Name/Date _____

Adjectives Related to Strength 2

Circle S for Synonyms or A for Antonyms to identify each word pair.

S A   1. robust/hearty
S A   2. sturdy/fragile
S A   3. thriving/flourishing
S A   4. burly/brawny
S A   5. muscular/puny

Name/Date _____

Adjectives Related to Strength 3

Shade the bubble beside the synonym for the first word in each line.

1. delicate: ◯ stalwart   ◯ intense   ◯ frail
2. fragile: ◯ flimsy   ◯ sturdy   ◯ invincible
3. faint: ◯ faded   ◯ loud   ◯ intense
4. puny: ◯ robust   ◯ muscular   ◯ scrawny
5. forceful: ◯ defenseless   ◯ powerful   ◯ ineffectual

Name/Date _____

Adjectives Related to Strength 4

On your own paper, use both synonyms from each pair in a sentence.

1. muscular/brawny
2. intense/strong
3. frail/delicate
4. puny/fragile
5. invincible/indestructible

Name/Date _____

Adjectives Related to Strength 5

Fill in the antonym's missing letters.

1. vulnerable   i _ v _ nci _ le
2. invulnerable   su _ ce _ t _ ble
3. invincible   b _ ata _ l _
4. impenetrable   pe _ m _ _ ble
5. untouchable   vu _ _ era _ _ e

Synonyms and Antonyms Warm-ups: Part I Qualities; Adjectives Related to Beauty

Name/Date _____

Adjectives Related to Beauty 1

Circle the antonym for the first word in each line.

1. beautiful: hideous   attractive   gorgeous
2. pretty: stunning   unattractive   appealing
3. ugly: repulsive   unsightly   lovely
4. pleasant: obnoxious   likeable   agreeable
5. charming: likeable   delightful   unappealing

Name/Date _____

Adjectives Related to Beauty 2

Unscramble the synonym for each word.
1. unappealing   atnactivtrue _____
2. gorgeous   rnikstig _____
3. stunning   lautecspcar _____
4. lovely   ntigenchan _____
5. attractive   dshaonme _____

Name/Date _____

Adjectives Related to Beauty 3

Circle S for Synonyms or A for Antonyms to identify each word pair.

S A   1.   handsome/unattractive

S A   2.   picturesque/quaint

S A   3.   scenic/lovely

S A   4.   delightful/unpleasant

S A   5.   unpleasant/disagreeable

Name/Date _____

Adjectives Related to Beauty 4

Fill in the synonym's missing letters.
1. hideous   re __ ugn __ nt
2. alluring   en __ hr __ __ l __ __ g
3. repulsive   ab __ or __ e __ t
4. dazzling   in __ red __ __ le
5. unattractive   u __ sig __ tly

Name/Date _____

Adjectives Related to Beauty 5

Circle T for True or F for False.

T F   1.   A *forbidding* cabin is *attractive*.

T F   2.   An *unsightly* chair is *gorgeous*.

T F   3.   A *charismatic* speaker is *alluring*.

T F   4.   A *revolting* insect is *stunning*.

T F   5.   A *magnificent* ballroom is *dazzling*.

Synonyms and Antonyms Warm-ups: Part I Qualities; Adjectives Related to Similarity

Name/Date _____

Adjectives Related to Similarity 1

Circle S for Synonyms or A for Antonyms to identify each word pair.

S A   1.   equivalent/comparable
S A   2.   equal/uneven
S A   3.   alike/different
S A   4.   comparable/similar
S A   5.   parallel/analogous

Name/Date _____

Adjectives Related to Similarity 2

Circle T for True or F for False.

T F   1.   If two ideas are *analogous*, they are *comparable*.

T F   2.   If one song is *akin* to another, they are *similar*.

T F   3.   If two shirts are *dissimilar*, they are *alike*.

T F   4.   If one son is *unlike* his brother, the two boys are *different*.

Name/Date _____

Adjectives Related to Similarity 3

Unscramble the antonym for each word.

1.   unrelated   levreant _____
2.   related   ctencuneond _____
3.   distinct   geuva _____
4.   unusual   ndmanue _____
5.   original   natiuiagivnme _____

Name/Date _____

Adjectives Related to Similarity 4

Fill in each synonym's missing letters.

1.   unique   e _ c _ _ ti _ n _ l
2.   diverse   va _ io _ s
3.   atypical   un _ ha _ act _ ris _ ic
4.   uncommon   _ n _ _ ual
5.   bizarre   p _ c _ l _ ar

Name/Date _____

Adjectives Related to Similarity 5

Circle the synonym for the first word in each line.

1.   same: identical   divergent   dissimilar
2.   different: equivalent   akin   unlike
3.   like: unrelated   resembling   distinct
4.   identical: original   unique   duplicate
5.   similar: comparable   uncommon   bizarre

Synonyms and Antonyms Warm-ups: Part I Qualities; Adjectives Related to Sound and Color

Name/Date _____

Sound and Color Adjectives 1

Match the synonyms.

_____ 1. high   a. muted
_____ 2. deep   b. lofty
_____ 3. shrill   c. bass
_____ 4. soft   d. thunderous
_____ 5. loud   e. piercing

Name/Date _____

Sound and Color Adjectives 2

Write the synonym for each word.

1. crimson _____
2. golden _____
3. lilac _____
4. emerald _____
5. ultramarine _____

Choices: blue, amber, green, ruby, purple

Name/Date _____

Sound and Color Adjectives 3

Cross out the choice that is not a synonym for the first word in each line.

1. red: crimson   scarlet   turquoise
2. yellow: golden   emerald   amber
3. green: magenta   lime   olive
4. blue: cerulean   azure   verdant
5. purple: indigo   lavender   amethyst

Name/Date _____

Sound and Color Adjectives 4

Unscramble the synonym for each word.

1. red   acltrse _____
2. yellow   fafnros _____
3. green   tusrearche _____
4. purple   aeumv _____
5. blue   odingi _____

Name/Date _____

Sound and Color Adjectives 5

Fill in the synonym's missing letters.

1. brown   um _ e _
2. blue   ce _ ul _ an
3. orange   pu _ _ k _ n
4. black   e _ on _
5. yellow   m _ _ ta _ d

Synonyms and Antonyms Warm-ups: Part I Qualities; Adjectives Related to the Sense of Touch

Name/Date _____

Sense of Touch Adjectives 1

Circle the antonym for the first word in each line.

1.	soft:	dry	hot	hard
2.	rough:	smooth	coarse	bumpy
3.	fluffy:	solid	feathery	downy
4.	slick:	slippery	greasy	dry
5.	shiny:	glossy	dull	burnished

Name/Date _____

Sense of Touch Adjectives 2

Match the synonyms.

_____ 1. glossy   a. fiery
_____ 2. furry   b. rough
_____ 3. bumpy   c. frosty
_____ 4. hot   d. shiny
_____ 5. cold   e. fuzzy

Name/Date _____

Sense of Touch Adjectives 3

Cross out the choice that is not a synonym to the first word in each line.

1. sticky: sultry   arid
2. dry: parched   soaked
3. wet: desiccated   sodden
4. damp: dry   clammy
5. soaked: parched   saturated

Name/Date _____

Sense of Touch Adjectives 4

Circle S for Synonym or A for Antonym to identify each word pair.

S A 1. metallic/polished
S A 2. silky/coarse
S A 3. glassy/rough
S A 4. prickly/spiny
S A 5. sticky/gummy

Name/Date _____

Sense of Touch Adjectives 5

Unscramble the synonym for each word.

1. hot   seltingerw _____
2. cold   ilclhy _____
3. icy   laalcgi _____
4. slippery   cliks _____
5. thick   uoiscvs _____

Synonyms and Antonyms Warm-ups: Part I Qualities; Adjectives Related to Smell and Taste

Name/Date _____

_____

Smell and Taste Adjectives 1

Circle the synonym for each word.

1. ripe: ready
              stale
              musty

2. rotten: putrid
              minty
              floral

3. stale: fresh
              crisp
              old

4. spoiled: tainted
              healthy
              delicious

5. fresh: dried
              stale
              crisp

Name/Date _____

Smell and Taste Adjectives 2

Circle *synonyms* or *antonyms* to identify each word pair.

1. sweet/saccharine   synonyms   antonyms
2. sour/tart   synonyms   antonyms
3. salty/briny   synonyms   antonyms
4. bitter/sweet   synonyms   antonyms
5. stale/fresh   synonyms   antonyms

Name/Date _____

Smell and Taste Adjectives 3

Write *true* or *false* for each statement.

1. A *floral* scent is *flowery*. _____
2. A *musty* scent is *fresh*. _____
3. A *perfumed* scent is *fragrant*. _____
4. A *strong* scent is *faint*. _____

Name/Date _____

Smell and Taste Adjectives 4

On your own paper, use each pair of antonyms in a sentence.

1. juicy/dry
2. delicious/tasteless
3. spicy/mild
4. sizzling/icy

Name/Date _____

Smell and Taste Adjectives 5

Fill in the synonym's missing letters.

1. dank   c _ a _ _ y
2. stuffy   s _ f _ o _ _ ti _ g
3. fragrant   ar _ ma _ _ c
4. putrid   r _ t _ _ n
5. acrid   pun _ e _ t

Synonyms and Antonyms Warm-ups: Part I Qualities; Adjectives Related to Appearance

Name/Date _____

Adjectives Related to Appearance 1

Match the antonyms.

_____ 1. clean   a. straight
_____ 2. clear   b. drab
_____ 3. colorful   c. dirty
_____ 4. crinkled   d. cloudy
_____ 5. crooked   e. smooth

Name/Date _____

Adjectives Related to Appearance 2

Circle S for Synonyms or A for Antonyms to identify each word pair.

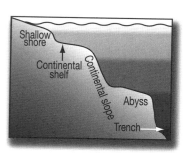

S   A   1. dim/bright
S   A   2. distinct/dissimilar
S   A   3. dull/bright
S   A   4. elegant/stylish
S   A   5. fancy/plain

Name/Date _____

Adjectives Related to Appearance 3

Circle the antonym for the first word in each line.

1. crowded: teeming   congested   deserted
2. curved: angular   rounded   curled
3. cute: adorable   ugly   appealing
4. dark: light   shadowy   obscure
5. deep: abysmal   unfathomable   shallow

Name/Date _____

Adjectives Related to Appearance 4

Write the correct antonym for each word.

1. filthy _____
2. flat _____
3. fluffy _____
4. foggy _____
5. glossy _____

Choices: clear, hard, hilly, dull, clean

Name/Date _____

Adjectives Related to Appearance 5

Circle T for True or F for False.

T   F   1. A *glamorous* movie star is *plain.*
T   F   2. A *gleaming* car is *dull.*
T   F   3. A *filthy* room is *dirty.*
T   F   4. A *graceful* dancer is *clumsy.*
T   F   5. A *grotesque* insect is *ugly.*

Synonyms and Antonyms Warm-ups: Part I Qualities; Adjectives Related to Appearance

Name/Date _____

Adjectives Related to Appearance 6

Match the antonyms.

_____ 1. hazy   a. beautiful

_____ 2. high   b. low

_____ 3. hollow   c. clear

_____ 4. homely   d. dark

_____ 5. light   e. solid

Name/Date _____

Adjectives Related to Appearance 7

Unscramble the synonym for each word.

1. muddy   cuykm _____
2. murky   adoyshw _____
3. narrow   hitn _____
4. oblique   dsantle _____
5. rotund   udrno _____

Name/Date _____

Adjectives Related to Appearance 8

Fill in the synonym's missing letters.

1. round   c __ r __ __ l __ r
2. pale   pal __ __ d
3. poised   c __ __ fi __ e __ t
4. quaint   pi __ tu __ __ sq __ e
5. shadowy   gl __ __ m __

Name/Date _____

Adjectives Related to Appearance 9

Write the correct antonym for each word.

1. shady _____
2. shallow _____
3. sheer _____
4. shiny _____
5. appealing _____

Choices: unattractive, dull, sunny, deep, opaque

Name/Date _____

Adjectives Related to Appearance 10

Circle the antonym for the first word in each line.

1. light: high   heavy   moving
2. lithe: stiff   clear   muddy
3. low: beautiful   high   foggy
4. misty: steamy   clear   slender
5. motionless: moving   frozen   hazy

Synonyms and Antonyms Warm-ups: Part I Qualities; Mixed Review

Name/Date _____

Qualities: Mixed Review 1

Match the synonyms.

_____ 1. amber   a. green

_____ 2. amethyst   b. yellow

_____ 3. chartreuse   c. blue

_____ 4. crimson   d. purple

_____ 5. azure   e. red

Name/Date _____

Qualities: Mixed Review 2

Circle S for Synonyms or A for Antonyms to identify each word pair.

S A   1. obstinate/stubborn

S A   2. normal/unusual

S A   3. noisy/quiet

S A   4. molten/liquefied

S A   5. primitive/sophisticated

Name/Date _____

Qualities: Mixed Review 3

Circle the synonym for the first word in each line.

1. ebony:	azure	verdant	black
2. ivory:	black	white	ochre
3. mint:	orange	yellow	green
4. lilac:	aqua	purple	ebony
5. ruby:	red	orange	olive

Name/Date _____

Qualities: Mixed Review 4

Fill in the synonym's missing letters.

1. quaint   o _ d-f _ _ hi _ _ _ e _

2. notable   im _ or _ _ _ n _

3. obvious   ap _ _ r _ nt

4. prominent   in _ lu _ nt _ al

5. persistent u _ r _ l _ nti _ _

Name/Date _____

Qualities: Mixed Review 5

Write the correct antonym for each word.

1. unique _____

2. feeble _____

3. preoccupied _____

4. rigid _____

5. rugged _____

Choices: flexible, powerful, smooth, focused, common

Synonyms and Antonyms Warm-ups: Part II Locations; Relative Position

Relative Position 1

Circle the antonym for the first word in each line.

1. from: higher   above   to
2. higher: back   lower   toward
3. lower: under   higher   between
4. backward: after   through   forward
5. nearer: farther   between   among

Name/Date _____

Relative Position 2

Write the correct antonym for each word.
1. up _____
2. above _____
3. below _____
4. toward _____
5. within _____

Choices: outside, below, down, above, away

Name/Date _____

Relative Position 3

Write *synonyms* or *antonyms* to identify each word pair.

1. over/above _____
2. above/below _____
3. neither/either _____
4. before/after _____
5. in/out _____

Name/Date _____

Relative Position 4

Unscramble the antonym.

1. against   orf _____
2. beneath   ebavo _____
3. with   uitwoht _____
4. to   rmof _____
5. behind   efeobr _____

Name/Date _____

Relative Position 5

Circle T for True or F for False.

T F 1. A store that is *farther* away is *closer*.

T F 2. A yard in the *back* is *behind* the house.

T F 3. A man *amid* a crowd is *among* many people.

T F 4. A *subsequent* act takes place *before* the first action.

Synonyms and Antonyms Warm-ups: Part II Locations; Relative Position

Name/Date _____

Relative Position 6

Write *synonyms* or *antonyms* to identify each word pair.
1. back/rear _____
2. below/beneath _____
3. divide/separate _____
4. in/out _____
5. inside/outside _____

Name/Date _____

Relative Position 7

Match the antonyms.
- ___ 1. north
- ___ 2. beneath
- ___ 3. toward
- ___ 4. this
- ___ 5. these

a. that
b. away
c. those
d. south
e. above

Name/Date _____

Relative Position 8

Write *true* or *false* for each statement.
1. *Opposite* walls are *beside* each other. _____
2. *Adjacent* walls are *beside* each other. _____
3. If a rock is *beside* a stream, it is *in* the water. _____
4. A *left-handed* person writes with his *right* hand. _____
5. If a frog sits *upon* a lily pad, he is on *top* of it. _____

Name/Date _____

Relative Position 9

Unscramble the antonym for each word.
1. close — stntadi _____
2. far — eran _____
3. top — otombt _____
4. highest — lsowet _____
5. inside — iduotse _____

Name/Date _____

Relative Position 10

Circle the antonym for each word.

1. near: between / above / far
2. now: then / far / below
3. on: through / off / too
4. here: there / through / above
5. east: north / south / west

Synonyms and Antonyms Warm-ups: Part III Emotions; Adverbs Related to Feelings

Name/Date _____

Adverbs Related to Feelings 1

Circle the synonym for the word in each line.

1. intently: powerfully   faintly   slowly
2. certainly: quietly   surely   nervously
3. tenderly: roughly   questioningly   gently
4. anxiously: admiringly   nervously   quickly
5. rebelliously: obediently   loyally   disobediently

Name/Date _____

Adverbs Related to Feelings 2

Unscramble the synonym for each word.

1. devotedly   alllyyo _____
2. inquisitively ucuslrioy _____
3. uniquely   iaplsecly _____
4. admiringly   glprovyapin

5. dynamically   asttialicehusnly

Name/Date _____

Adverbs Related to Feelings 3

Match the synonyms.

_____ 1. sadly   a. blissfully
_____ 2. excitedly   b. bravely
_____ 3. tenaciously   c. persistently
_____ 4. happily   d. dejectedly
_____ 5. courageously   e. feverishly

Certificate of Bravery

Name/Date _____

Adverbs Related to Feelings 4

Circle S for Synonyms or A for Antonyms to identify each word pair.

S A   1. warmly/heartlessly
S A   2. curiously/peculiarly
S A   3. boldly/adventurously
S A   4. securely/unsafely
S A   5. touchingly/poignantly

Name/Date _____

Adverbs Related to Feelings 5

Write the correct antonym for each word.

1. bravely _____
2. sympathetically _____
3. daringly _____
4. vaguely _____
5. defiantly _____

Choices: definitely, fearfully, unkindly, respectfully, cautiously

Synonyms and Antonyms Warm-ups: Part III Emotions; Adjectives Related to Feelings

Name/Date _____

Adjectives Related to Feelings 1

Match the synonyms.

_____ 1. cheerful   a. relieved

_____ 2. impulsive   b. engrossed

_____ 3. interested   c. sympathetic

_____ 4. concerned   d. blithe

_____ 5. reassured   e. rash

Name/Date _____

Adjectives Related to Feelings 2

Write *synonyms* or *antonyms* to identify each word pair.

1. strong/infirm _____
2. loving/affectionate _____
3. merry/sorrowful _____
4. eager/ambitious _____
5. bright/somber _____

Name/Date _____

Adjectives Related to Feelings 3

Circle the antonym for the first word in each line.

1. elated:	joyful	depressed	intelligent
2. keen:	interested	unenthusiastic	sharp
3. loving:	adoring	sympathetic	antagonistic
4. sunny:	gloomy	cheerful	delightful
5. positive:	assured	confident	negative

Name/Date _____

Adjectives Related to Feelings 4

Write the correct synonym for each word.
1. considerate _____
2. affected _____
3. jubilant _____
4. free _____
5. affectionate _____

Choices: unfettered, touched, devoted, exuberant, attentive

Name/Date _____

Adjectives Related to Feelings 5

Cross out the choice that is not an antonym for the first word in the line.

1. fascinated: bored   spellbound
2. earnest: fervent   insincere
3. sure: dubious   definite
4. sensitive: feeling   uncaring
5. intrigued: captivated
                 uninterested

Synonyms and Antonyms Warm-ups: Part III Emotions; Adjectives Related to Feelings

Name/Date _____

_____

Adjectives Related to Feelings 6

Circle the synonym for each word.

1. satisfied: content
                miserable
                disgruntled
2. thankful: ungracious
                churlish
                grateful
3. frisky: lackluster
                spirited
                dreary
4. content: unhappy
                comfortable
                uneasy
5. receptive: approachable
                imprisoned
                despondent

Name/Date _____

Adjectives Related to Feelings 7

Match the antonyms.

_____ 1. clever	a. despondent
_____ 2. interested	b. unaffected
_____ 3. gleeful	c. imprisoned
_____ 4. free	d. indifferent
_____ 5. shocked	e. foolish

Name/Date _____

Adjectives Related to Feelings 8

Write the correct antonym for each word.

1. important _____
2. animated _____
3. quiet _____
4. arrogant _____
5. festive _____

Choices:
lethargic
humble
gloomy
trivial
boisterous

Name/Date _____

Adjectives Related to Feelings 9

Circle S for Synonyms or A for Antonyms.

S A   1. spirited/energetic
S A   2. certain/unsure
S A   3. kind/benevolent
S A   4. ecstatic/wretched
S A   5. thrilled/delighted

Name/Date _____

Adjectives Related to Feelings 10

Fill in the chart with a synonym and antonym for each word.

	Synonym	Antonym
1. relaxed	_____	_____
2. taciturn	_____	_____
3. meek	_____	_____
4. exhilarated	_____	_____

Synonyms and Antonyms Warm-ups: Part III Emotions; Adjectives Related to Angry Emotions

Name/Date _____

Angry Emotions Adjectives 1

Write *synonyms* or *antonyms* to identify each word pair.

1. angry/calm _____
2. annoyed/irritated _____
3. mad/furious _____
4. arrogant/humble _____
5. outraged/shocked _____

Name/Date _____

Angry Emotions Adjectives 2

Unscramble the synonym for each word.

1. resentful   eedmterbit _____
2. vindictive   usmioalic _____
3. bullying   edoinngmeri _____
4. callous   insivitnsee _____
5. heartless   nlmostiesoe _____

NO BULLYING

Name/Date _____

Angry Emotions Adjectives 3

Fill in the antonym's missing letters.

1. cruel   c __ __ pa __ __ io __ ate
2. mean   s __ __ p __ __ he __ __ c
3. cross   a __ r __ e __ __ le
4. inconsiderate   th __ __ g __ __ f __ l
5. insensitive   re __ pon __ __ ve

Name/Date _____

Angry Emotions Adjectives 4

Circle T for True or F for False.

T F   1. A *terse* statement is *wordy.*

T F   2. A *sharp* answer is *angry.*

T F   3. A *harsh* reply is *polite.*

T F   4. A *nasty* response is *disagreeable.*

T F   5. An *evil* act is *vile.*

Name/Date _____

Angry Emotions Adjectives 5

Circle two synonyms for the first word in each line.

1. furious: cheerful   raging   angry
2. aggressive: hostile   bold   mild
3. combative: agreeable   quarrelsome   pugnacious
4. belligerent: antagonistic   controlled   combative
5. hostile: unfriendly   amicable   ornery

Synonyms and Antonyms Warm-ups: Part III Emotions; Adjectives Related to Sad Emotions

Name/Date _____

Sad Emotions Adjectives 1

Circle the synonym for the first word in each line.

1. abandoned: deserted   crowded   treasured
2. dejected: cheerful   delighted   crestfallen
3. alone: solitary   congested   swarming
4. deserted: inhabited   populated   uninhabited
5. desolate: barren   populous   busy

TOWN 2 Miles

Name/Date _____

Sad Emotions Adjectives 2

Unscramble the antonym for each word.

1. alienated   voinelvd _____
2. miserable   ligtedehd _____
3. sad   usyjoo _____
4. bored   eiastnsithuc _____
5. despondent   ijlova _____

Name/Date _____

Sad Emotions Adjectives 3

Fill in the synonym's missing letters.

1. downcast   di _ _ ap _ _ in _ ed
2. excluded   di _ qu _ _ if _ _ d
3. estranged   a _ i _ na _ _ d
4. crushed   s _ a _ _ er _ d
5. despised   l _ at _ _ _ d

Name/Date _____

Sad Emotions Adjectives 4

Circle S for Synonyms or A for Antonyms to identify each word pair.

S   A   1. lonesome/friendless
S   A   2. lonely/isolated
S   A   3. grieving/celebratory
S   A   4. forlorn/cheerful
S   A   5. humiliated/dishonored

Name/Date _____

Sad Emotions Adjectives 5

Write *true* or *false* for each statement.

1. If you are *depressed*, you are *happy*. _____
2. If you are *glum,* you are *gloomy.* _____
3. A *grim* situation is *dismal.* _____
4. If a friend looks *forlorn,* she looks *dejected.* _____
5. If someone is *loathed,* he is *loved.* _____

Synonyms and Antonyms Warm-ups: Part III Emotions; Adjectives Related to Fearful Emotions

Name/Date _____

Fearful Emotions Adjectives 1

Circle S for Synonyms or A for Antonyms for each word pair.

S A   1. afraid/terrified
S A   2. anxious/worried
S A   3. alarmed/untroubled
S A   4. jumpy/tranquil
S A   5. nervous/tense

Name/Date _____

Fearful Emotions Adjectives 2

Circle the synonym for the first word in each line.
1. terrified: petrified   comfortable   embarrassed
2. timid: excited   hopeful   reticent
3. shy: thrilled   bashful   comfortable
4. uneasy: apprehensive   confident   trustful
5. uncomfortable: contented   composed   awkward

Name/Date _____

Fearful Emotions Adjectives 3

On your own paper, write sentences using both antonyms in each word pair.

1. fearful/fearless   2. bashful/confident
3. embarrassed/proud   4. intimidated/sure
5. shaky/steady

Name/Date _____

Fearful Emotions Adjectives 4

Unscramble the synonyms for each word.
1. tense   ensipapevreh _____
2. insecure   abevunrlel _____
3. hesitant   veentatit _____
4. frantic   nfrizdee _____

Name/Date _____

Fearful Emotions Adjectives 5

Write *true* or *false* for each statement.

1. If you are *upset,* you are *troubled.*

    _____

2. If you are *scared,* you are *timorous.*

    _____

3. If you are *restless,* you are *agitated.*

    _____

4. If you are *jittery,* you are *serene.*

    _____

5. If you are *horrified,* you are *delighted.*

    _____

Synonyms and Antonyms Warm-ups: Part III Emotions; Adjectives Related to Happy Emotions

Name/Date _____

Happy Emotions Adjectives 1

Circle the antonym for the first word in each line.

1. glad: gleeful   unhappy   cheerful
2. enthusiastic: apathetic   eager   anxious
3. contented: unsatisfied pleased   cheerful
4. ecstatic: delighted   miserable   joyful
5. excited: agitated   energized   bored

Name/Date _____

Happy Emotions Adjectives 2

Write *synonyms* or *antonyms* to identify each word pair.

1. joyful/ecstatic _____
2. happy/miserable _____
3. cheerful/blithe _____
4. amused/bored _____
5. delighted/dismayed _____

Name/Date _____

Happy Emotions Adjectives 3

Unscramble the synonym for each word.

1. funny   hmuoruos _____
2. witty   cevrel _____
3. humorous   ccailom _____
4. jolly   crhyee _____
5. hilarious uraurioops _____

Name/Date _____

Happy Emotions Adjectives 4

Match the antonyms.

_____ 1. pleased   a. disappointed
_____ 2. pleasant   b. modest
_____ 3. friendly   c. disagreeable
_____ 4. satisfied   d. unhappy
_____ 5. proud   e. unfriendly

Name/Date _____

Happy Emotions Adjectives 5

Circle T for True or F for False.

T F 1. If a student is *relieved*, he is *worried*.
T F 2. If an actor is *thrilled*, he is *pleased*.
T F 3. If an athlete is *triumphant*, she is *victorious*.
T F 4. If a cat is *satisfied*, it is *content*.
T F 5. If a contestant is *ecstatic*, she is *unhappy*.

Synonyms and Antonyms Warm-ups: Part III Emotions; Adjectives Related to Loving Emotions

Name/Date _____

Loving Emotions Adjectives 1

Unscramble the synonym for each word.

1. adorable   lvlaboe _____
2. caring   ndik _____
3. concerned   rdwrieo _____
4. loving   afoatnfectie _____
5. warm   neyldfri _____

Name/Date _____

Loving Emotions Adjectives 2

On your own paper, use each word pair in a sentence.

1. cordial/pleasant
2. congenial/unfriendly
3. genuine/real
4. helpful/harmful
5. good/worthy

Name/Date _____

Loving Emotions Adjectives 3

Write the correct synonym for each word.

1. altruistic _____
2. benign _____
3. considerate _____
4. honorable _____
5. optimistic _____

> **Choices:** admirable, hopeful, kind, unselfish, thoughtful

Name/Date _____

Loving Emotions Adjectives 4

Fill in the synonym's missing letters.

1. tolerant   u __ d __ rs __ a __ __ i __ g
2. sympathetic   co __ __ __ ss __ __ n __ te
3. mellow   s __ re __ __
4. empathetic   sy __ __ a __ __ __ tic
5. courteous   po __ __ t __

Name/Date _____

Loving Emotions Adjectives 5

Find and circle an antonym for each word in the puzzle at right.

1. lovable
2. kind
3. just
4. generous
5. forgiving

Z	H	N	H	S	I	F	L	E	S
C	F	P	Z	M	Z	M	X	P	V
L	M	N	L	R	R	X	Q	Q	S
M	Q	N	U	X	D	N	T	L	S
B	U	N	F	A	I	R	J	L	E
J	K	Z	E	Q	M	M	R	L	L
J	K	N	T	K	K	T	E	K	I
N	G	B	A	R	Y	U	M	R	T
K	M	L	H	X	R	Q	R	Y	I
M	R	C	P	C	M	J	D	H	P

Synonyms and Antonyms Warm-ups: Part III Emotions; Review of Adjectives Related to Emotions

Name/Date _____

Review of Emotion Adjectives 1

Circle the antonym for each word.

1. gloomy: cheery
             glum
             miserable
2. greedy: selfish
             voracious
             generous
3. healthy: unhealthy
             fit
             robust
4. jolly: cheerful
             miserable
             happy
5. nasty: unpleasant
             disgusting
             agreeable

Name/Date _____

Review of Emotion Adjectives 2

Match the synonyms.

____ 1. able	a.	benevolent
____ 2. lively	b.	active
____ 3. thankful	c.	skilled
____ 4. kind	d.	nervous
____ 5. tense	e.	grateful

Name/Date _____

Review of Emotion Adjectives 3

Circle S for Synonyms or A for Antonyms for each word pair.

S A   1. timid/bold
S A   2. loyal/faithful
S A   3. afraid/frightened
S A   4. arrogant/humble
S A   5. brave/courageous

Name/Date _____

Review of Emotion Adjectives 4

Circle T for True or F for False for each statement.

T F   1. If a man is *cautious,* he is *reckless.*
T F   2. *Crazy* actions are *sensible.*
T F   3. If your friend is *busy,* she is *occupied.*
T F   4. If a neighbor is *generous,* she is *selfish.*
T F   5. If your uncle is *gentle,* he is *brutal.*

Name/Date _____

Review of Emotion Adjectives 5

Write the synonym.

1. naïve _____
2. wise _____
3. rude _____
4. relaxed _____
5. tragic _____

Choices:
disastrous
sensible
serene
innocent
impolite

Synonyms and Antonyms Warm-ups: Part III Emotions; Review of Adjectives Related to Emotions

Name/Date _____

Review of Emotion Adjectives 6

Match the antonyms.

_____ 1. innocent   a. serious
_____ 2. tolerant   b. doubting
_____ 3. playful   c. guilty
_____ 4. calm   d. anxious
_____ 5. confident   e. unforgiving

Name/Date _____

Review of Emotion Adjectives 7

Write the correct synonym for each word.

1. courageous _____
2. peaceful _____
3. reliable _____
4. joyous _____
5. energetic _____

Choices: tranquil, jubilant, lively, trustworthy, brave

Name/Date _____

Review of Emotion Adjectives 8

Circle the antonym for the first word in each line.

1. easy: difficult   simple
2. lucky: fortunate   unfortunate
3. liberated: released   imprisoned
4. cozy: uncomfortable   snug
5. amazed: astonished   unsurprised

Name/Date _____

Review of Emotion Adjectives 9

Unscramble the synonym for each word.

1. fortunate   ucykl _____
2. optimistic   olpehuf _____
3. pleased   tiasdsfie _____
4. free   peindnndeet _____
5. delighted   vyoederjo _____

Name/Date _____

Review of Emotion Adjectives 10

Fill in the blank with a synonym to the italicized word that correctly completes each sentence.

1. The *provocative* gestures of the lion tamer were only mildly _____ to the lazy lion.
2. *Encouraged* by her friends, the girl was _____ to enter the contest.
3. *Overjoyed* when she won the contest, Brenda remained _____ for days.
4. The _____ decision was *impulsive* and not well thought out.

Choices: ecstatic, irritating, motivated, rash

Synonyms and Antonyms Warm-ups: Part III Emotions; Review of Adverbs Related to Emotions

Name/Date _____

Review of Emotion Adverbs 1

Find and circle an antonym for each word in the puzzle at right.

1. comfortably
2. hastily
3. calmly
4. carefully
5. fondly

W	Y	D	J	F	B	R	H	W	L	K	Y	Y
M	L	N	E	R	V	O	U	S	L	Y	V	Z
M	B	Z	H	R	R	Y	G	Y	L	Y	H	N
T	A	C	F	B	M	F	Q	F	L	R	A	W
R	T	K	A	W	V	B	C	L	D	M	T	C
X	R	N	T	R	D	K	U	N	F	C	E	T
K	O	K	D	N	E	F	Q	D	W	J	F	K
L	F	Z	P	G	E	L	L	Y	Q	T	U	W
X	M	N	M	R	K	K	E	D	Z	M	L	W
B	O	B	A	D	T	L	T	S	F	H	L	L
X	C	C	R	Z	K	Q	T	P	S	M	Y	D
H	N	D	N	X	Q	L	C	N	H	L	M	R
K	U	F	T	M	T	V	Y	N	N	K	Y	P

Name/Date _____

Review of Emotion Adverbs 2

Circle S for Synonyms or A for Antonyms to identify each word pair.

S A   1. happily/sadly
S A   2. sadly/miserably
S A   3. wearily/energetically
S A   4. miserably/poorly
S A   5. angrily/furiously

Name/Date _____

Review of Emotion Adverbs 3

Unscramble the synonym for each word.

1. energetically   tilvacey _____
2. vivaciously   orolviusgy _____
3. glumly   olmigloy _____
4. cheerfully   eyrirml _____
5. delightedly   ulglfeyle _____

Name/Date _____

Review of Emotion Adverbs 4

Match the antonyms.

_____ 1. respectfully   a. closely
_____ 2. recklessly   b. roughly
_____ 3. remotely   c. unscrupulously
_____ 4. gently   d. rudely
_____ 5. honorably   e. cautiously

Name/Date _____

Review of Emotion Adverbs 5

Circle the antonym for the first word in each line.

1. hesitantly: cautiously   decisively
2. kindly: unkindly   gently
3. gently: softly   brutally
4. warmly: lovingly   coldly
5. icily: coolly   hotly

Synonyms and Antonyms Warm-ups: Part III Emotions; Review of Adverbs Related to Emotions

Name/Date _____

Review of Emotion Adverbs 6

Circle S for Synonyms or A for Antonyms to identify each word pair.

S A 1. shamefully/proudly
S A 2. adoringly/lovingly
S A 3. admiringly/disapprovingly
S A 4. confidently/assertively
S A 5. annoyingly/gratifyingly

Name/Date _____

Review of Emotion Adverbs 7

Match the antonyms.

_____ 1. awkwardly   a. sharply
_____ 2. beautifully   b. sweetly
_____ 3. bitterly   c. selfishly
_____ 4. bluntly   d. gracefully
_____ 5. generously   e. hideously

Name/Date _____

Review of Emotion Adverbs 8

Circle the antonym for the first word in each line.

1. silently: quietly   stealthily   noisily
2. sensibly: foolishly   wisely   prudently
3. shyly: meekly   confidently   fearfully
4. boldly: timidly   bravely   brazenly
5. laughingly: jokingly   tearfully   playfully

Name/Date _____

Review of Emotion Adverbs 9

Write the correct antonym for each word.
1. powerfully _____
2. playfully _____
3. optimistically _____
4. obviously _____
5. peacefully _____

Choices: seriously, violently, mysteriously, weakly, pessimistically

Name/Date _____

Review of Emotion Adverbs 10

Unscramble the synonym for each word.
1. triumphantly   uioorysltvic
_____
2. enthusiastically sitelayonpas
_____
3. fearfully   preseaheivnply
_____
4. frantically   elradpetesy
_____

Synonyms and Antonyms Warm-ups: Part IV Actions; Synonyms and Antonyms for Verbs

Name/Date _____

Actions: Verbs 1 Cross out the choice that is not a synonym for the first word in each line.

1.	eat:	cook	consume	devour
2.	achieve:	accomplish	fail	attain
3.	allow:	refuse	permit	grant
4.	ask:	declare	question	interrogate
5.	astonish:	surprise	amaze	harangue

Name/Date _____

Actions: Verbs 2 Write the correct synonym for each word.

1. begin _____
2. call _____
3. close _____
4. consent _____
5. continue _____

Choices:
persevere
shut
agree
initiate
yell

Name/Date _____

Actions: Verbs 3 Circle two synonyms for the first word in each line.

1. cure: heal   harm   restore
2. decrease: increase   lessen   diminish
3. divide: separate   unite   split
4. dwell: live   reside   depart
5. delay: postpone   procrastinate   hasten

Name/Date _____

Actions: Verbs 4 Match the synonyms.

a. depart   b. elucidate   c. develop   d. complete   e. repair

_____ 1. end
_____ 3. fix
_____ 5. grow
_____ 2. explain
_____ 4. go

Name/Date _____

Actions: Verbs 5 Circle T for True or F for False for each statement.

T F   1. If you *hate* cucumbers, you *detest* them.   T F   2. If you *have* a bike, you *possess* it.

T F   3. If you *assist* someone, you *hinder* his progress.

T F   4. When you *conceal* a fact, you *uncover* it.   T F   5. If you *grasp* a handle, you *clutch* it.

Synonyms and Antonyms Warm-ups: Part IV Actions; Synonyms and Antonyms for Verbs

Name/Date _____

Actions: Verbs 6

Write *synonyms* or *antonyms* to identify each word pair.

1. injure/wound _____
2. keep/release _____
3. last/endure _____
4. depart/arrive _____
5. enjoy/loathe _____

Name/Date _____

Actions: Verbs 7

Write the correct synonym for each word.

1. learn _____
2. listen _____
3. look _____
4. make _____
5. mend _____

Choices: construct, hear, restore, understand, glance

Name/Date _____

Actions: Verbs 8

Match the synonyms.

_____ 1. move   a. delete
_____ 2. need   b. unseal
_____ 3. occur   c. transport
_____ 4. omit   d. require
_____ 5. open   e. happen

Name/Date _____

Actions: Verbs 9

Cross out the choice that is not a synonym for the first word in each line.

1. outlive: survive halt outlast
2. pardon: accuse excuse forgive
3. praise: applaud compliment criticize
4. prohibit: allow forbid stop
5. put: take locate place

Name/Date _____

Actions: Verbs 10

Fill in the blank with an antonym to the italicized word that correctly completes each sentence.

Choices: act, begin, compose, defend, end

1. While the coyotes *raided* the camp, the dog tried to _____ the children.
2. Don't just *say* you will help, do something to _____ on your promise.
3. Sally will _____ her essay, and then she will edit and *revise* it.
4. The *start* of the race is five kilometers from the _____.
5. At noon we will *halt* for lunch, and then we'll _____ hiking again at one o'clock.

Synonyms and Antonyms Warm-ups: Part IV Actions; Synonyms and Antonyms for Verbs

Name/Date _____

Actions: Verbs 11

Cross out the choice that is not a synonym for the first word in each line.

1. take: give   grab   seize
2. terrify: frighten   soothe   alarm
3. thaw: melt   dissolve   freeze
4. think: act   contemplate reflect
5. try: quit   endeavor   attempt

Name/Date _____

Actions: Verbs 12

Write the correct synonym for each word.

1. understand _____
2. unify _____
3. urge _____
4. use _____
5. walk _____

Choices: consolidate, stroll, exhort, comprehend, employ

Name/Date _____

Actions: Verbs 13

Circle the synonym for the first word in each line.

1. verify: confirm   deny
2. write: speak   record
3. achieve: fail   succeed
4. add: decrease   increase
5. admire: respect   detest

Name/Date _____

Actions: Verbs 14

Match the antonyms.

_____ 1. accept   a. hate
_____ 2. adore   b. hinder
_____ 3. advance   c. reject
_____ 4. affirm   d. retreat
_____ 5. help   e. deny

Name/Date _____

Actions: Verbs 15

Write the correct antonym for each word.

1. break _____
2. attack _____
3. annoy _____
4. arrive _____
5. bend _____

Choices: straighten, repair, depart, defend, soothe

Synonyms and Antonyms Warm-ups: Part IV Actions; Synonyms and Antonyms for Verbs

Name/Date _____

Actions: Verbs 16

Match the antonyms.

_____ 1. build
_____ 2. bring
_____ 3. buy
_____ 4. capture
_____ 5. close

a. remove
b. release
c. destroy
d. open
e. sell

Name/Date _____

Actions: Verbs 17

Write *synonyms* or *antonyms* to identify each word pair.

1. stay/leave _____
2. cry/weep _____
3. damage/break _____
4. create/destroy _____
5. unite/join _____

Name/Date _____

Actions: Verbs 18

Circle the antonym for the first word in each line.

1. end: stop halt begin
2. expand: shrink enlarge grow
3. fail: pass lose collapse
4. succeed: win fail triumph
5. gain: get lose acquire

Name/Date _____

Actions: Verbs 19

Write the correct antonym for each word.
1. get _____
2. give _____
3. guess _____
4. go _____
5. attack _____

Choices: know, give, come, protect, receive

Name/Date _____

Actions: Verbs 20

Unscramble the antonym for each word.

1. hate oevl _____
2. hurt ephl _____
3. keep osle _____
4. leave vareri _____
5. mix sraeepat _____

Synonyms and Antonyms Warm-ups: Part IV Actions; Synonyms and Antonyms for Verbs

Name/Date _____

_____

Actions: Verbs 21

Circle the antonym for each word.

1. boil: freeze
             heat
             bubble

2. bury: hide
             cover
             unearth

3. connect: join
             separate
             combine

4. arrive: appear
             come
             depart

5. answer: ask
             respond
             react

Name/Date _____

Actions: Verbs 22

Circle S for Synonyms or A for Antonyms for each word pair.

S A   1. annoy/please
S A   2. borrow/lend
S A   3. discover/find
S A   4. explain/clarify
S A   5. extend/reduce

Name/Date _____

Actions: Verbs 23

Match the synonyms.

_____ 1. fit   a. creep
_____ 2. hope   b. act
_____ 3. crawl   c. place
_____ 4. cure   d. heal
_____ 5. behave   e. expect

Name/Date _____

Actions: Verbs 24

Unscramble the synonym for each word.

1. command   rdroe _____
2. flap   abte _____
3. desert   aanndob _____
4. deserve   ertmi _____
5. complete   nhisfi _____

Name/Date _____

Actions: Verbs 25

Fill in the antonym's missing letters

1. attract   r _ p _ l
2. compliment   i _ s _ l _
3. brake   a _ _ el _ ra _ _
4. thaw   fr _ _ z _
5. remain   d _ p _ _ t

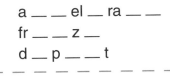

Synonyms and Antonyms Warm-ups: Part IV Actions; Synonyms and Antonyms for Verbs

Name/Date _____

Actions: Verbs 26

Match the synonyms.

_____ 1. disappear   a. utilize

_____ 2. hover   b. vanish

_____ 3. identify   c. recognize

_____ 4. deceive   d. trick

_____ 5. use   e. float

Name/Date _____

Actions: Verbs 27

Write the correct synonym for each word.

1. copy _____

2. fix _____

3. attempt _____

4. damage _____

5. decay _____

Choices:
try
repair
deteriorate
harm
reproduce

Name/Date _____

Actions: Verbs 28

Circle the antonym for the first word in each line.

1. wash: dry   cleanse   scrub

2. ignore: notice   disregard   overlook

3. destroy: demolish   construct   wreck

4. detect: notice   discover   conceal

5. harm: injure   heal   hurt

Name/Date _____

Actions: Verbs 29

Unscramble the synonym for each word.

1. head   mmdanco _____

2. excuse   rdnpao _____

3. fade   nahisv _____

4. disagree   oratdcicnt _____

5. harass   nyoan _____

Name/Date _____

_____

Actions: Verbs 30

Find and circle a synonym for each word in the puzzle below.

1. want

2. warm

3. romp

4. prohibit

5. move

M	W	E	H	L	F	T	P	J	T
R	K	R	T	K	F	F	X	R	X
W	M	I	H	N	N	Q	A	L	G
J	R	S	K	P	R	N	G	M	F
F	T	E	N	T	S	K	D	N	D
K	O	D	K	P	F	T	N	D	C
Z	W	R	O	D	A	P	L	A	Y
N	P	R	B	E	G	M	M	X	W
L	T	B	H	I	R	W	F	Q	M
N	K	T	W	R	D	Q	K	W	K

Synonyms and Antonyms Warm-ups: Part IV Actions; Synonyms and Antonyms for Verbs

Name/Date _____

Actions: Verbs 31

Match the synonyms.

_____ 1. joke   a. tie

_____ 2. knot   b. tease

_____ 3. launch   c. teach

_____ 4. fit   d. belong

_____ 5. instruct   e. start

Name/Date _____

Actions: Verbs 32

Write the correct synonym for each word.

1. look _____
2. mark _____
3. endure _____
4. join _____
5. grab _____

Choices: persist, seize, connect, glance, label

Name/Date _____

Actions: Verbs 33

Unscramble the synonym for each word.

1. gaze   unscetiizr _____
2. like   ynjoe _____
3. mix   cbneiom _____
4. pack   rawp _____
5. release   refe _____

Name/Date _____

Actions: Verbs 34

Fill in the antonym's missing letters.

1. attach   re _ _ _ se
2. make   d _ _ t _ _ y
3. prohibit   a _ _ _ w
4. sit   _ _ _ n _
5. command   o _ _ y

Name/Date _____

Actions: Verbs 35

Circle the antonym for the first word in each line.

1. please: delight   displease   cheer
2. multiply: add   increase   divide
3. urge: deter   coax   encourage
4. offer: refuse   give   suggest
5. precede: lead   follow   act

Synonyms and Antonyms Warm-ups: Part IV Actions; Synonyms and Antonyms for Verbs

Name/Date _____

Actions: Verbs 36

Write the correct synonym for each word.

1. change _____
2. grip _____
3. happen _____
4. fetch _____
5. intend _____

> **Choices:** retrieve, grasp, plan, alter, occur

Name/Date _____

Actions: Verbs 37

Fill in the synonym's missing letters.

1. describe   r __ p __ __ t
2. wail   c __ __
3. reign   r __ __ e
4. sack   d __ st __ __ y
5. pause   h __ s __ __ __ te

Name/Date _____

Actions: Verbs 38

Circle the synonym for the first word in each line.

1. pretend: imagine   prove   haunt
2. interfere: ignore   include   intrude
3. permit: forbid   allow   restrict
4. heap: flatten   lower   pile
5. include: contain   exclude   prohibit

Name/Date _____

Actions: Verbs 39

Unscramble the synonym for each word.

1. waver   ctatuflue _____
2. verify   cromnfi _____
3. work   olit _____
4. terrify   fhngtrie _____
5. sell   envd _____

Name/Date _____

Actions: Verbs 40

Write *synonyms* or *antonyms* to identify each word pair.

1. rejoice/regret _____
2. show/demonstrate _____
3. supply/provide _____
4. continue/interrupt _____
5. assist/aid _____

Synonyms and Antonyms Warm-ups: Part IV Actions; Synonyms and Antonyms for Verbs

Name/Date _____

Actions: Verbs 41

Circle the hidden synonym in each line.

1. help   hiddenassistretreatwalkdeiverimpress
2. amaze   tyrwstponmbaerspinawayastonishdodge
3. receive   seelaendobtainansatowrfknpincelonly
4. punish   penalizerewardgivetriumphcommend
5. question   replyanswerreplaceinquirelloosenlisten

Name/Date _____

Actions: Verbs 42

Match the antonyms.

_____ 1. found   a. loosen
_____ 2. guard   b. listen
_____ 3. tighten   c. lost
_____ 4. discourage   d. attack
_____ 5. call   e. encourage

Name/Date _____

Actions: Verbs 43

Write the correct synonym for each word.

1. deliver _____
2. walk _____
3. form _____
4. grin _____
5. change _____

Choices: bring, saunter, shape, smile, transform

Name/Date _____

Actions: Verbs 44

Write *synonyms* or *antonyms* to identify each word pair.

1. remember/forget _____
2. work/play _____
3. begin/end _____
4. wish/desire _____
5. shiver/tremble _____

Name/Date _____

Actions: Verbs 45

Circle the synonym for the first word in each line.

1. teach: instruct   learn   study
2. observe: deliver   punish   examine
3. promise: desire   vow   require
4. remain: depart   exit   linger
5. repair: break   mend   shatter

Synonyms and Antonyms Warm-ups: Part V Items; Synonyms and Antonyms for Nouns

---

Name/Date _____

Items: Nouns 1   Circle the hidden synonym in each line.

1. children   sheetyoungsterspublicstory
2. car   methodvehicleclamoruproartop
3. city   donationmetropolisblundertumult
4. country   citycountycontinenttownnation

Name/Date _____

Items: Nouns 2   Write the correct synonym for each word.

1. method _____   2. mistake _____
3. noise _____   4. ornament _____
5. page _____

Choices:
decoration
sheet
technique
blunder
clamor

Name/Date _____

Items: Nouns 3   Match the synonyms.

   a. occupation   b. concept   c. rubbish   d. solution   e. present

_____ 1. gift   _____ 2. idea
_____ 3. job   _____ 4. junk
_____ 5. key

Name/Date _____

Items: Nouns 4   Write *synonyms* or *antonyms* to identify each word pair.

1. ache/hurt _____   2. summit/base _____
3. people/public _____   4. story/tale _____
5. strength/weakness _____

Name/Date _____

Items: Nouns 5   Unscramble the synonym for each word.

1. thief   obrrbe _____   2. gratitude   preiiatnoapc _____
3. tumult   hsaco _____   4. victor   mphiocan _____
5. wealth   neturfo _____

Synonyms and Antonyms Warm-ups: Part V Items; Synonyms and Antonyms for Nouns

Name/Date _____

Items: Nouns 6

Circle S for Synonyms or A for Antonyms to identify each word pair.

S A   1. work/play
S A   2. accomplishment/failure
S A   3. amateur/professional
S A   4. child/youngster
S A   5. world/earth

Name/Date _____

Items: Nouns 7

Match the antonyms.

_____ 1. child   a. sky
_____ 2. compliment   b. enemy
_____ 3. friend   c. adult
_____ 4. day   d. insult
_____ 5. earth   e. night

Name/Date _____

Items: Nouns 8

Write the correct antonym for each word.

1. evening _____
2. evil _____
3. failure _____
4. fiction _____
5. friend _____

Choices: fact, enemy, morning, good, success

Name/Date _____

Items: Nouns 9

Circle the antonym for the first word in each line.

1. ground: dirt   floor   sky
2. head: foot   top   ceiling
3. height: level   depth   ground
4. liquid: wet   milk   solid
5. hero: winner champion coward

Name/Date _____

Items: Nouns 10

Circle the hidden antonym in each line.

1. hill   mountainvalleyrollingsolid
2. individual   onlyalonegroupsingleunique
3. male   manboydrakefemaleroosterbull
4. woman   femalegirlduckhenmothermanteacher
5. father   womanmanfemalemalegroupmother

Synonyms and Antonyms Warm-ups: Part V Items; Synonyms and Antonyms for Nouns

Name/Date _____

Items: Nouns 11

Match the antonyms.

_____ 1. sister   a. disturbance

_____ 2. peace   b. teacher

_____ 3. play   c. humility

_____ 4. pupil   d. work

_____ 5. pride   e. brother

Name/Date _____

Items: Nouns 12

Write the correct antonym for each word.

1. profit _____
2. superiority _____
3. problem _____
4. right _____
5. apprentice _____

Choices: solution, loss, wrong, master, inferiority

Name/Date _____

Items: Nouns 13

Find and circle the antonym for each word in the puzzle at the right.

1. shack
2. light
3. shame
4. silence
5. friend

X	F	K	D	F	X	M	T	Y	M
K	E	L	F	O	P	M	H	Z	M
M	C	B	M	E	C	X	R	N	N
R	A	N	W	M	M	N	L	Q	Q
C	L	N	R	E	P	R	I	D	E
Q	A	N	D	J	S	L	V	N	N
N	P	A	Y	D	L	O	Z	R	C
T	H	R	T	F	B	C	U	X	H
S	Z	N	K	R	K	G	H	N	Y
D	N	N	T	R	G	R	Y	F	D

Name/Date _____

Items: Nouns 14

Unscramble the antonym for each word.

1. truth   fdehaools _____
2. hero   lnlavii _____
3. host   etsgu _____
4. defeat   hmtiurp _____
5. top   siudnrdee _____

Name/Date _____

Items: Nouns 15

On your own paper, use each pair of antonyms in a sentence.

1. ceiling/floor
2. light/dark
3. sea/land
4. motion/stillness
5. liquid/solid

Synonyms and Antonyms Warm-ups: Part V Items; Synonyms and Antonyms for Nouns

Name/Date _____

_____

Items: Nouns 16

Circle the synonym for the first word in each line.

1. money: barter
            currency
            poverty
2. picture: illustration
            text
            transcript
3. lumber: steel
            wood
            aluminum
4. beach: seashore
            ornament
            ocean
5. puzzle: answer
            riddle
            solution

Name/Date _____

Items: Nouns 17

Match the antonyms.

_____ 1. beginner   a. suburb
_____ 2. afternoon   b. famine
_____ 3. downtown   c. morning
_____ 4. daughter   d. expert
_____ 5. feast   e. son

Name/Date _____

Items: Nouns 18

Write the correct synonym for each word.

1. apparel _____
2. creature _____
3. crate _____
4. graveyard _____

Choices:
cemetery
animal
clothing
container

Name/Date _____

Items: Nouns 19

Circle T for True or F for False for each statement.

T F 1. If a man has a *fortune,* he has *wealth.*
T F 2. A *stranger* is always a *friend.*
T F 3. *Punishment* is better than a *reward.*
T F 4. *Mortification* is a feeling of *shame.*
T F 5. *Pain* is not as enjoyable as *pleasure.*

Name/Date _____

Items: Nouns 20

Write *synonyms* or *antonyms* to identify each word pair.

1. quiet/tranquility _____
2. recess/break _____
3. activity/inactivity _____
4. beggar/philanthropist _____
5. passenger/traveler _____

Synonyms and Antonyms Warm-ups: Part V Items; Synonyms and Antonyms for Nouns

Name/Date _____

Items: Nouns 21

Circle the synonym for the first word in each line.

1.	territory:	creature	hopelessness	land
2.	route:	way	carrot	chase
3.	scent:	sound	vision	smell
4.	textile:	feeling	roughness	cloth
5.	attorney:	lawyer	instructor	physician

Name/Date _____

Items: Nouns 22

Match the synonym.

_____ 1. mitten   a. chair

_____ 2. voyage   b. riches

_____ 3. wealth   c. author

_____ 4. writer   d. glove

_____ 5. throne   e. trip

Name/Date _____

Items: Nouns 23

Write the correct antonym for each word.

1. health _____

2. fire _____

3. poison _____

4. daughter _____

5. visitor _____

Choices: medicine, son, resident, illness, smoke

Name/Date _____

Items: Nouns 24

Fill in the synonym's missing letters.

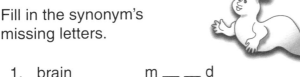

1. brain   m __ __ d

2. beast   __ n __ __ al

3. ghost   s __ __ r __ __

4. bucket   p __ __ __

5. scene   __ l __ __ e

Name/Date _____

Items: Nouns 25

On your own paper, write sentences using the synonym or antonym word pairs.

1. battle/combat

2. cellar/basement

3. ocean/land

4. hope/aspiration

5. afterthought/forethought

Answer Keys

Part I: Qualities
Adjectives Related to Size (p. 2)
Exercise 1
1. little
2. diminutive
3. gigantic
4. typical
5. large

Exercise 2
1. extreme
2. tiny
3. gigantic
4. minuscule
5. small

Exercise 3
1. middle
2. little
3. massive
4. immense
5. minuscule

Exercise 4
Answers will vary. Example: There was a *minute* insect on the *enormous* elephant's back.

Exercise 5
Cross out:
1. minuscule
2. microscopic
3. infinitesimal
4. diminutive
5. mammoth

Adjectives Related to Shape (p. 3)
Exercise 1
1. circular
2. boxy
3. thin
4. thick
5. level

Exercise 2
1. round
2. cubic
3. plump
4. spherical
5. bowed

Exercise 3
1. quadrilateral
2. globular
3. blocky
4. slim
5. narrow

Exercise 4
1. antonyms
2. synonyms
3. synonyms
4. antonyms

Exercise 5
1. F
2. F
3. F
4. T
5. T

Adjectives Related to Age (p. 4)
Exercise 1
1. synonyms
2. synonyms
3. antonyms
4. synonyms
5. antonyms

Exercise 2
Answers will vary.

Exercise 3
1. current
2. contemporary
3. unfashionable
4. traditional
5. primeval

Exercise 4
1. ancient
2. modern
3. damaged
4. advanced
5. unoriginal

Exercise 5
1. latest
2. improved
3. ancient
4. outmoded
5. antiquated

Adjectives Related to Strength (p. 5)
Exercise 1
Cross out:
1. vigorous
2. feeble
3. forceful
4. extreme
5. listless

Exercise 2
1. S
2. A
3. S
4. S
5. A

Exercise 3
1. frail
2. flimsy
3. faded
4. scrawny
5. powerful

Exercise 4
Answers will vary.

Exercise 5
1. invincible
2. susceptible
3. beatable
4. permeable
5. vulnerable

Adjectives Related to Beauty (p. 6)
Exercise 1
1. hideous
2. unattractive
3. lovely
4. obnoxious
5. unappealing

Exercise 2
1. unattractive
2. striking
3. spectacular
4. enchanting
5. handsome

Exercise 3
1. A
2. S
3. S
4. A
5. S

Exercise 4
1. repugnant
2. enthralling
3. abhorrent
4. incredible
5. unsightly

Exercise 5
1. F
2. F
3. T
4. F
5. T

Adjectives Related to Similarity (p. 7)
Exercise 1
1. S
2. A
3. A
4. S
5. S

Exercise 2
1. T
2. T
3. F
4. T

Exercise 3
1. relevant
2. unconnected
3. vague
4. mundane
5. unimaginative

Exercise 4
1. exceptional
2. various
3. uncharacteristic
4. unusual
5. peculiar

Exercise 5
1. identical
2. unlike
3. resembling
4. duplicate
5. comparable

Adjectives Related to Sound and Color (p. 8)
Exercise 1
1. b
2. c
3. e
4. a
5. d

Exercise 2
1. ruby
2. amber
3. purple
4. green
5. blue

Exercise 3
Cross out:
1. turquoise
2. emerald
3. magenta
4. verdant
5. indigo

Exercise 4
1. scarlet
2. saffron
3. chartreuse
4. mauve
5. indigo

Exercise 5
1. umber
2. cerulean
3. pumpkin
4. ebony
5. mustard

Adjectives Related to the Sense of Touch (p. 9)
Exercise 1
1. hard
2. smooth
3. solid
4. dry
5. dull

Exercise 2
1. d
2. e
3. b
4. a
5. c

Exercise 3
1. arid
2. soaked
3. desiccated
4. dry
5. parched

Exercise 4
1. S
2. A
3. A
4. S
5. S

Exercise 5
1. sweltering
2. chilly
3. glacial
4. slick
5. viscous

Adjectives Related to Smell and Taste (p. 10)
Exercise 1
1. ready
2. putrid
3. old
4. tainted
5. crisp

Exercise 2
1. synonyms
2. synonyms
3. synonyms
4. antonyms
5. antonyms

Exercise 3
1. true
2. false
3. true
4. false

Exercise 4
Answers will vary.

Exercise 5
1. clammy   2. suffocating
3. aromatic   4. rotten
5. pungent

Adjectives Related to Appearance (p. 11)

Exercise 1
1. c   2. d   3. b   4. e   5. a

Exercise 2
1. A   2. S   3. A   4. S   5. A

Exercise 3
1. deserted   2. angular
3. ugly   4. light
5. shallow

Exercise 4
1. clean   2. hilly   3. hard
4. clear   5. dull

Exercise 5
1. F   2. F   3. T   4. F   5. T

Adjectives Related to Appearance (p. 12)

Exercise 6
1. c   2. b   3. e   4. a   5. d

Exercise 7
1. mucky   2. shadowy
3. thin   4. slanted
5. round

Exercise 8
1. circular   2. pallid
3. confident   4. picturesque
5. gloomy

Exercise 9
1. sunny   2. deep
3. opaque   4. dull
5. unattractive

Exercise 10
1. heavy   2. stiff   3. high
4. clear   5. moving

Qualities: Mixed Review (p. 13)

Exercise 1
1. b   2. d   3. a   4. e   5. c

Exercise 2
1. S   2. A   3. A   4. S   5. A

Exercise 3
1. black   2. white   3. green
4. purple   5. red

Exercise 4
1. old-fashioned   2. important
3. apparent   4. influential
5. unrelenting

Exercise 5
1. common   2. powerful
3. focused   4. flexible
5. smooth

Part II: Locations
Relative Position (p. 14)

Exercise 1
1. to   2. lower   3. higher
4. forward 5. farther

Exercise 2
1. down   2. below   3. above
4. away   5. outside

Exercise 3
1. synonyms   2. antonyms
3. antonyms   4. antonyms
5. antonyms

Exercise 4
1. for   2. above
3. without   4. from   5. before

Exercise 5
1. F   2. T   3. T   4. F

Relative Position (p. 15)

Exercise 6
1. synonyms   2. synonyms
3. synonyms   4. antonyms
5. antonyms

Exercise 7
1. d   2. e   3. b   4. a   5. c

Exercise 8
1. false   2. true   3. false
4. false   5. true

Exercise 9
1. distant   2. near   3. bottom
4. lowest   5. outside

Exercise 10
1. far   2. then   3. off
4. there   5. west

Part III: Emotions
Adverbs Related to Feelings (p. 16)

Exercise 1
1. powerfully   2. surely
3. gently   4. nervously
5. disobediently

Exercise 2
1. loyally   2. curiously
3. specially   4. approvingly
5. enthusiastically

Exercise 3
1. d   2. e   3. c   4. a   5. b

Exercise 4
1. A   2. S   3. S   4. A   5. S

Exercise 5
1. fearfully   2. unkindly
3. cautiously   4. definitely
5. respectfully

Adjectives Related to Feelings (p. 17)

Exercise 1
1. d   2. e   3. b   4. c   5. a

Exercise 2
1. antonyms   2. synonyms
3. antonyms   4. synonyms
5. antonyms

Exercise 3
1. depressed   2. unenthusiastic
3. antagonistic 4. gloomy
5. negative

Exercise 4
1. attentive   2. touched
3. exuberant   4. unfettered
5. devoted

Exercise 5
Cross out: 1. spellbound
2. fervent   3. definite
4. feeling   5. captivated

Adjectives Related to Feelings (p. 18)

Exercise 6
1. content   2. grateful
3. spirited   4. comfortable
5. approachable

Exercise 7
1. e   2. d   3. a   4. c   5. b

Exercise 8
1. trivial   2. lethargic
3. boisterous   4. humble
5. gloomy

Exercise 9
1. S   2. A   3. S   4. A   5. S

Exercise 10
Answers will vary. Possible answers:
1. relaxed: calm, excited
2. taciturn: quiet, loud
3. meek: humble, arrogant
4. exhilarated: thrilled, miserable

Adjectives Related to Angry Emotions (p. 19)

Exercise 1
1. antonyms   2. synonyms
3. synonyms   4. antonyms
5. synonyms

Exercise 2
1. embittered   2. malicious
3. domineering   4. insensitive
5. emotionless

Exercise 3
1. compassionate
2. sympathetic 3. agreeable
4. thoughtful   5. responsive

Exercise 4
1. F   2. T   3. F   4. T   5. T

Exercise 5
1. raging, angry
2. hostile, bold
3. quarrelsome, pugnacious
4. antagonistic, combative
5. unfriendly, ornery

Adjectives Related to Sad Emotions (p. 20)

Exercise 1
1. deserted   2. crestfallen
3. solitary   4. uninhabited
5. barren

Exercise 2
1. involved   2. delighted
3. joyous   4. enthusiastic
5. jovial

Exercise 3
1. disappointed
2. disqualified 3. alienated
4. shattered   5. loathed

Exercise 4
1. S   2. S   3. A   4. A   5. S

Exercise 5
1. false   2. true   3. true
4. true   5. false

Adjectives Related to Fearful Emotions (p. 21)

Exercise 1
1. S   2. S   3. A   4. A   5. S

Exercise 2
1. petrified   2. reticent
3. bashful   4. apprehensive
5. awkward

Exercise 3
Answers will vary.

Exercise 4
1. apprehensive   2. vulnerable
3. tentative   4. frenzied

Exercise 5
1. true   2. true   3. true
4. false   5. false

Adjectives Related to Happy Emotions (p. 22)

Exercise 1
1. unhappy   2. apathetic
3. unsatisfied   4. miserable
5. bored

Exercise 2
1. synonyms   2. antonyms
3. synonyms   4. antonyms
5. antonyms

Exercise 3
1. humorous   2. clever
3. comical   4. cheery
5. uproarious

Exercise 4
1. d   2. c   3. e   4. a   5. b

Exercise 5
1. F   2. T   3. T   4. T   5. F

Adjectives Related to Loving Emotions (p. 23)

Exercise 1
1. lovable   2. kind
3. worried   4. affectionate
5. friendly

Exercise 2
Answers will vary.

Exercise 3
1. unselfish   2. kind
3. thoughtful   4. admirable
5. hopeful

Exercise 4
1. understanding
2. compassionate   3. serene
4. sympathetic   5. polite

Exercise 5
1. hateful   2. cruel   3. unfair
4. selfish   5. pitiless

Review of Adjectives Related to Emotions (p. 24)

Exercise 1
1. cheery   2. generous
3. unhealthy   4. miserable
5. agreeable

Exercise 2
1. c   2. b   3. e   4. a   5. d

Exercise 3
1. A   2. S   3. S   4. A   5. S

Exercise 4
1. F   2. F   3. T   4. F   5. F

Exercise 5
1. innocent   2. sensible
3. impolite   4. serene
5. disastrous

Review of Adjectives Related to Emotions (p. 25)

Exercise 6
1. c   2. e   3. a   4. d   5. b

Exercise 7
1. brave   2. tranquil
3. trustworthy   4. jubilant
5. lively

Exercise 8
1. difficult   2. unfortunate
3. imprisoned   4. uncomfortable
5. unsurprised

Exercise 9
1. lucky   2. hopeful
3. satisfied   4. independent
5. overjoyed

Exercise 10
1. irritating   2. motivated
3. ecstatic   4. rash

Review of Adverbs Related to Emotions (p. 26)

Exercise 1
1. uncomfortably   2. carefully
3. nervously   4. carelessly
5. hatefully

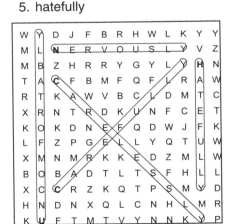

Exercise 2
1. A   2. S   3. A   4. S   5. S

Exercise 3
1. actively   2. vigorously
3. gloomily   4. merrily
5. gleefully

Exercise 4
1. d 2. e 3. a 4. b 5. c
Exercise 5
1. decisively 2. unkindly
3. brutally 4. coldly 5. hotly

Review of Adverbs Related to Emotions (p. 27)
Exercise 6
1. A 2. S 3. A 4. S 5. A
Exercise 7
1. d 2. e 3. b 4. a 5. c
Exercise 8
1. noisily 2. foolishly
3. confidently 4. timidly
5. tearfully
Exercise 9
1. weakly 2. seriously
3. pessimistically
4. mysteriously 5. violently
Exercise 10
1. victoriously 2. passionately
3. apprehensively
4. desperately

Part IV: Actions
Synonyms and Antonyms for Verbs (p. 28)
Exercise 1
Cross out: 1. cook
2. fail 3. refuse
4. declare 5. harangue
Exercise 2
1. initiate 2. yell 3. shut
4. agree 5. persevere
Exercise 3
1. heal, restore
2. lessen, diminish
3. separate, split
4. live, reside
5. postpone, procrastinate
Exercise 4
1. d 2. b 3. e 4. a 5. c
Exercise 5
1. T 2. T 3. F 4. F 5. T

Synonyms and Antonyms for Verbs (p. 29)
Exercise 6
1. synonyms 2. antonyms
3. synonyms 4. antonyms
5. antonyms
Exercise 7
1. understand 2. hear
3. glance 4. construct
5. restore

Exercise 8
1. c 2. d 3. e 4. a 5. b
Exercise 9
1. halt 2. accuse
3. criticize 4. allow 5. take
Exercise 10
1. defend 2. act 3. compose
4. end 5. begin

Synonyms and Antonyms for Verbs (p. 30)
Exercise 11
Cross out: 1. give 2. soothe
3. freeze 4. act 5. quit
Exercise 12
1. comprehend 2. consolidate
3. exhort 4. employ 5. stroll
Exercise 13
1. confirm 2. record
3. succeed 4. increase
5. respect
Exercise 14
1. c 2. a 3. d 4. e 5. b
Exercise 15
1. repair 2. defend
3. soothe 4. depart
5. straighten

Synonyms and Antonyms for Verbs (p. 31)
Exercise 16
1. c 2. a 3. e 4. b 5. d
Exercise 17
1. antonyms 2. synonyms
3. synonyms 4. antonyms
5. synonyms
Exercise 18
1. begin 2. shrink 3. pass
4. fail 5. lose
Exercise 19
1. give 2. receive 3. know
4. come 5. protect
Exercise 20
1. love 2. help 3. lose
4. arrive 5. separate

Synonyms and Antonyms for Verbs (p. 32)
Exercise 21
1. freeze 2. unearth
3. separate 4. depart
5. ask
Exercise 22
1. A 2. A 3. S 4. S 5. A
Exercise 23
1. c 2. e 3. a 4. d 5. b

Exercise 24
1. order 2. beat
3. abandon 4. merit
5. finish
Exercise 25
1. repel 2. insult
3. accelerate 4. freeze
5. depart

Synonyms and Antonyms for Verbs (p. 33)
Exercise 26
1. b 2. e 3. c 4. d 5. a
Exercise 27
1. reproduce 2. repair
3. try 4. harm 5. deteriorate
Exercise 28
1. dry 2. notice
3. construct 4. conceal
5. heal
Exercise 29
1. command 2. pardon
3. vanish 4. contradict
5. annoy
Exercise 30
1. desire 2. heat 3. play
4. forbid 5. transport

Synonyms and Antonyms for Verbs (p. 34)
Exercise 31
1. b 2. a 3. e 4. d 5. c
Exercise 32
1. glance 2. label 3. persist
4. connect 5. seize
Exercise 33
1. scrutinize 2. enjoy
3. combine 4. wrap
5. free
Exercise 34
1. release 2. destroy
3. allow 4. stand 5. obey

Jumpstarters for Energy Technology

Exercise 35
1. displease   2. divide
3. deter   4. refuse   5. follow

Synonyms and Antonyms for Verbs (p. 35)

Exercise 36
1. alter   2. grasp   3. occur
4. retrieve   5. plan

Exercise 37
1. report   2. cry   3. rule
4. destroy   5. hesitate

Exercise 38
1. imagine   2. intrude
3. allow   4. pile
5. contain

Exercise 39
1. fluctuate   2. confirm
3. toil   4. frighten
5. vend

Exercise 40
1. antonyms   2. synonyms
3. synonyms   4. antonyms
5. synonyms

Synonyms and Antonyms for Verbs (p. 36)

Exercise 41
1. assist   2. astonish
3. obtain   4. penalize
5. inquire

Exercise 42
1. c   2. d   3. a   4. e   5. b

Exercise 43
1. bring   2. saunter   3. shape
4. smile   5. transform

Exercise 44
1. antonyms   2. antonyms
3. antonyms   4. synonyms
5. synonyms

Exercise 45
1. instruct   2. examine
3. vow   4. linger   5. mend

Part V: Items
Synonyms and Antonyms for Nouns (p. 37)

Exercise 1
1. youngsters   2. vehicle
3. metropolis   4. nation

Exercise 2
1. technique   2. blunder
3. clamor   4. decoration
5. sheet

Exercise 3
1. e   2. b   3. a   4. c   5. d

Exercise 4
1. synonyms   2. antonyms
3. synonyms   4. synonyms
5. antonyms

Exercise 5
1. robber   2. appreciation
3. chaos   4. champion
5. fortune

Synonyms and Antonyms for Nouns (p. 38)

Exercise 6
1. A   2. A   3. A   4. S   5. S

Exercise 7
1. c   2. d   3. b   4. e   5. a

Exercise 8
1. morning   2. good
3. success   4. fact
5. enemy

Exercise 9
1. sky   2. foot   3. depth
4. solid   5. coward

Exercise 10
1. valley   2. group   3. female
4. man   5. mother

Synonyms and Antonyms for Nouns (p. 39)

Exercise 11
1. e   2. a   3. d   4. b   5. c

Exercise 12
1. loss   2. inferiority
3. solution   4. wrong
5. master

Exercise 13
1. palace   2. shade   3. pride
4. sound   5. foe

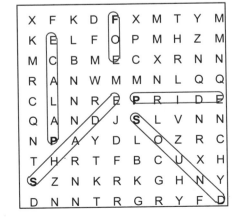

Exercise 14
1. falsehood   2. villain
3. guest   4. triumph
5. underside

Exercise 15
Answers will vary.

Synonyms and Antonyms for Nouns (p. 40)

Exercise 16
1. currency   2. illustration
3. wood   4. seashore
5. riddle

Exercise 17
1. d   2. c   3. a   4. e   5. b

Exercise 18
1. clothing   2. animal
3. container   4. cemetery

Exercise 19
1. T   2. F   3. F   4. T   5. T

Exercise 20
1. synonyms   2. synonyms
3. antonyms   4. antonyms
5. synonyms

Synonyms and Antonyms for Nouns (p. 41)

Exercise 21
1. land   2. way   3. smell
4. cloth   5. lawyer

Exercise 22
1. d   2. e   3. b   4. c   5. a

Exercise 23
1. illness   2. smoke
3. medicine   4. son
5. resident

Exercise 24
1. mind   2. animal
3. spirit   4. pail   5. place

Exercise 25
Answers will vary.